# NOW OR NEVER!

If you wish to scale the heights of your own potential, you must apply the adage of Socrates and, "Know Thyself." Success is a personal process. Yet, most theories of success fail to acknowledge every dimension of personal success. The Now or Never goal program will help you align who you are with what you want to achieve. This is accomplished by dividing the program into the 7 components of T.H.Y.S.E.L.F:

**Time:** How to go from being busy to being focused!

**Health:** How to have the energy to look and feel your best!

**Your Mind:** How to use your mind to yield positive results!

**Spirituality:** How to build belief and take action!

**Eternal Influence:** How to live and leave a legacy!

**Loving Relationships:** How to improve your relationships!

**Finance:** How to profit by strengthening your strengths!

# NOW OR NEVER!

### A STEP-BY-STEP
### SYSTEM FOR REACHING
### YOUR MOST IMPORANT GOAL
## IN 21 DAYS

## RYAN JEFFERY

**SPIRIT REIGN**
PUBLISHING
A Division of Spirit Reign Communications

# Now or Never!

Available from:

Spirit Reign Communications

www.spiritreign.org

256.759.7492

Author: Ryan Jeffery

Cover Design: Daryl S. Anderson Sr.

Page Layout & Design: Ornan Anthony of OA.Blueprints, LLC

Editor: Zaidie Crowe Carnegie

Printed in the United States of America.

ISBN# 978-0-9839323-0-7

**SPIRIT REIGN**
PUBLISHING
A Division of Spirit Reign Communications

# CONTENTS

# ACKNOWLEDGEMENTS

I thank Jesus Christ for giving me life and undeserved favor. He blessed me to meet, befriend, and marry Jarren Thurman Jeffery. Her love, talent, and partnership have strengthened me to help thousands of people improve their lives over the past 14 years. She inspires me to bring out the best in others by the way she brings out the best in me.

How fortunate I am to have entered this world with Harry and Myra Jeffery as parents. At every stage of childhood, they helped me see the relationship between my choices and circumstances. They achieved the balance between fostering independence and providing support. My beautiful sister Tia has always been more than a biological sibling. Her friendship, quiet strength, and sense of humor add joy to my life.

The professionalism, creativity, and partnership of Jeremy Anderson, Pastor Daryl Anderson, and the entire team at Spirit Reign Communications have proved a positive blessing. They are to be commended for their patience in dealing with my last minute changes while having to meet tight deadlines.

Finally, I want to thank Dave Levein Photography for supporting this project and helping me relax in front of the camera. Apart from the names mentioned, there are several family members, friends, colleagues, teachers, clients, mentors, church leaders, and students who have contributed to my understanding of goal achievement. Thank you all for being a part of my life!

Love,

Ryan

# INTRODUCTION

## EACH DAY IS A GIFT

It was an early Friday morning on November 11, 2011. I was driving to an elementary school to help a team develop behavior intervention strategies for a Kindergarten student. At 32 years of age, I was a behavior specialist for 11 different schools in my district. A normal day consisted of visiting five schools to coach teachers, consult administrators, meet with parents, model lessons, conduct staff training, type a report, and manage a demanding calendar. Each day was like a week of experience.

## YOUR LIFE CAN CHANGE IN A MOMENT

My vehicle was a refuge from the pressing needs that awaited me at each appointment. One day, I had a moment to reflect as I stopped in the left turning lane of a large intersection. After the arrow turned green, I made a left turn through the intersection. There was no sign of what was speeding around a curve across this intersection. A huge Chevy Silverado mashed the pedal to the floor when he saw his light turn yellow! By the time he reached the intersection, I was halfway into my turn. Within a split second, the grill of a huge truck was inches away from my passenger window. I clinched the steering wheel and yelled, "Jesus!" I felt a powerful impact shoot through my body as this Chevy Silverado bashed into my four door Lexus. For the next two seconds, time moved in slow motion. My car spun around the intersection as glass from my windows shattered everywhere. The sound was like a baseball bat smashing my windows . Thank God I was the only passenger. My wife would have normally been seated where the truck made direct impact! When the car stopped, I took the key out of the ignition and jumped out of my car. Thankfully, my legs came with me.

Next, I heard a voice shout, "Sir, you're bleeding and you're in shock. Stop walking around like that!" People who witnessed the accident immediately came to my defense. One man ran to the truck driver and started to curse him out for running a red light. Another gentleman provided me with tissue for my bleeding forehead and lip. Another man dialed 911. Meanwhile, I was looking for my cell phone to call my wife and rearrange the appointments I had for the day. After failing to locate my cell phone, I walked toward the Chevy Silverado and knocked on the passenger window. The driver rolled the window down and I said, "Man, you ran straight into me!" He bowed his head and spoke softly in a language that I didn't understand." Seconds later the police and firefighters rushed to the scene. The police documented our insurance information and started taking notes for a report.

## ADRENALINE

Our vehicles blocked half the intersection leading to the elementary school I was scheduled to visit. A commotion began to build as parents and buses were delayed en route to dropping off their students. A few teachers recognized me and sent word to the school. Meanwhile, firefighters and paramedics urged me to get into the ambulance. I kept repeating, "I need to get my work bag and cell phone!" They replied, "You're in shock sir, just calm down." This was only adding to my stress. Finally, a teacher approached the fireman and demanded, "Let the man have his bags. He has confidential documents in there!" As I'm being lifted into the ambulance, they brought my work bags into the vehicle. I heard my car being towed away as I drove off in the ambulance. All I thought of was, "where is my cell phone so I can call my wife?" How will I contact my next four appointments?" The reality of the accident and that I could have died was not fully registered.

On the way to the hospital the emergency staff checked my vitals and said everything looked good. They informed me that my seatbelt stopped me from flying through the windshield. No bones were broken. There were only two minor injuries: First, the side impact of the truck caused a lateral shift in my lower back. This would take months of physical therapy to correct. Second, my head hit the steering wheel and a piece of my lip was removed. When I arrived at Reston Hospital, they immediately took me in to be examined. The elementary school contacted my Supervisor at the District Administration building. Our administrative assistant called into my hospital room and helped to settle my anxiety. She told me that my Supervisor was on his way and she would call my wife at work. When I hung the phone, the emergency room staff escorted me into surgery for my lip. Afterwards, they took x-rays and began preparing my clearance to go home. Suddenly, my wife Jarren burst through the door with an anxious look on her face. She ran to hug me and asked, "Are you okay honey?" I replied, "I'm fine sweety, thanks for being here."

## GETTING MY PRIORITIES STRAIGHT

When my wife arrived, the reality of how fortunate I was started to kick in. We prayed together and thanked God for sparing my life. After being discharged, I checked the clock and realized there was time to make a few of my appointments that day. As we are walking out of the hospital I asked Jarren, "Would you mind taking me to Enterprise Car Rental?" My car had been towed after the accident but I believed that I still had time to make some of my appointments. Jarren looked at me like I was nuts. "Ryan, you need to go home!" On our way out, we met my Supervisor who had just arrived at the hospital. We had a discussion about the events around the accident. He was glad that I was okay and we appreciated his support. This provided my wife with the opportunity to team up with my Supervisor for support. She explained, "Ryan is trying to get a rental car and make the rest of his appointments today!" My Supervisor replied, "Don't even think about it. You need to go home, get some rest, and sort things through. Give me your appointment contacts and I will let them know you can't make it today." He further explained that the other Behavior Specialist in our department could help cover my schools if I needed a few days to sort things out.

Although my body was still pumped with adrenaline, I knew that Jarren and my Supervisor were correct. Besides, who can win a debate with two of their bosses? The fact that I even thought to finish my work day showed that my priorities were out of whack. How did I get to a place where I was starting to place urgency over importance? This went against the principles that were responsible for the success God allowed me to experience up to that point in my journey.

## LIVE EACH DAY LIKE IT'S YOUR LAST

I went to Church the next day and spent some time with my extended family. My heart was flooded with gratitude for having a chance to re-align my priorities and live according to God's plan. I use to take it for granted that I would see someone again. Now I realized that each moment with those I cared about was precious. What if that moment was my last opportunity to see them? My next realization was that I was putting off important tasks and subtly being dominated by urgent tasks. It was my personal conviction that God was prompting me to write and publish a book over the past few years. This car accident awoke me to the reality that opportunities can be cut short. Likewise, when you have an opportunity; it is meant to be seized now - You may never have the opportunity again!

## PERSPECTIVE ON YOUR PAST

After a near death experience, one tends to reflect on the past from a spiritual perspective. My entire life didn't flash before my eyes. However something just as unique happened over the next few days. It became clear to me that God had strategically placed opportunities in my path throughout life. There was no way that I could take credit for the unique circumstances that God caused to be a part of my life. Additionally, I began to realize that those opportunities were time sensitive. They were placed in my life at a particular time for a particular purpose.

## A SINNER'S PRAYER

As a high school student I was a Hip-Hop fanatic who created rap music and DJ'd several parties. At one point I won a freestyle contest on WKYS in Washington DC. My father was a professional Disc Jockey as a teenager and I was following in his footsteps. Momentum started to develop in my freshman year of college. I was going to either pursue this path or focus on my education. Strangely, at this time I worked in a bakery with an ex-drug dealer. He was studying to become a Minister. He would casually preach to me every day at work. Yet, his words didn't seem like preaching. He talked to me in a way that pierced my defensiveness. One day he persuaded me to sincerely pray to God about the direction of my life and His purpose for my existence. That day I was the last person to leave the bakery. I took his advice and poured my heart out in prayer while I was sweeping the floor. I talked to God the way one would speak to a real person but with complete honesty. I told Him that I loved Hip-Hop and didn't want to abandon my talent or popularity. For some reason, I decided to give God a try. I decided to walk in whatever path He revealed to me. After that prayer, I walked to my dorm room to take a nap.

## AWAKENED FROM MY SLEEP

I was awakened by a knock on the door. It was a Promoter of a Christian concert who was told that a DJ was living in the dorm. He knocked door to door until people directed him to my room. He asked if I would be willing to use my talents for a Christian Show and in a state of shock, I agreed. This was the first time I was ever asked to DJ for a Christian venue. This was a direct answer to a silent prayer that nobody knew I prayed! That Christian concert with that particular group of artists only happened once! It was a now or never moment. Connecting with that group started a chain of events that led me out of the Hip Hop World into a purpose that has brought me true joy and happiness. Sometimes I ask myself, "What if I never prayed that prayer?" I'm sure the Lord could have eventually reached me. However, the exact set of circumstances would never have presented themselves again. This Now or Never principle is also applicable to romantic relationships.

## WINDOWS OF OPPORTUNITY

My wife and I met in college during the only window of time we would have been in the same location. We had grown up in different States and we mingled in different social circles in our first three years of college. Yet, we became best friends during our senior year. Our relationship developed during a six month period that may never have occurred again. After graduation, she returned to New Jersey and I returned to Maryland. Our decision to get engaged was based on the friendship we developed in our last year of college. We were only twenty and twenty one years old. Consequently, I honored the tradition of meeting with her parents to discuss my intentions of marrying their daughter. That's a hard sell when you're fresh out of college without a, "real" job.

## GOD DOESN'T CALL THE PREPARED;
## HE PREPARES THE CALLED

We graduated during a time when school systems were offering college graduates the opportunity to enter the teaching field with a non-education degree. The contingency was that you had to complete your education courses within 3-5 years of full-time teaching. The goal was that Jarren and I would secure gainful employment and save money for our wedding.

## LOVE IS BLIND!

The day arrived for me to ask my potential in- laws to marry their youngest daughter. When I arrived, my fiancé was unusually silent. I joined her on one side of room while her parents sat on the other. As the conversation began, I explained how our friendship had developed to the point of us falling in love and wanting to be married. After a brief pause my fiancé's father looked at all of us and made a loud declaration: "Love is blind!" He pointed to his wife and said, "You see this woman right here? I've been looking at her for thirty four years! Are you ready for that?" We all laughed while his wife slapped him on the shoulder and said, "Louis hush." On a positive note, they believed that we had the potential to be a great couple. Yet, they had valid concerns about stable employment.

My future father- in- law asked me very detailed questions about my plans for employment. To make a long story short, I promised him that his daughter and I would have full-time jobs in the education field within the next month or so. This was a bold promise but it was a promise made in faith.

During the job seeking process, Jarren and I discovered how to reach our most important goal in 21-days. By God's grace, she was employed as an elementary math teacher and I was employed as a secondary special education teacher. We saved money to pay for a wedding and continued to progress in the education field.

## 21-DAY CYCLES

Over the next ten years, we began to realize that God placed opportunities in our path that had 21 day turnover periods.This held true in situations such as entering graduate school, buying a house, revitalizing church ministry departments, learning special skills to increase our income, restoring broken relationships, etc. I'm going to make you a bold promise. If you follow my directions for 21 days, you will not recognize your life a month from today! The momentum you gain from reaching your most important goal will set the stage for an exciting lifestyle! You are being presented with an opportunity that God has placed in your path for such a time as this! God's purposes knows no haste or delay. In the larger scheme of things, His goals will always be accomplished. The question is this: Will you be a part of it?

The Now or Never Goal Program will help you take small steps that will make a big difference! Adressing each area of T.H.Y.S.E.L.F. will bridge personal gaps that are neglected in the traditional S.M.A.R.T approach to goal setting.

# HAVE YOU ASKED T.H.Y.S.E.L.F.
# THE FOLLWING QUESTIONS?

1. Time: How do I create the time to reach my goals when I'm pulled in so many different directions?

2. Health: How do I look and feel my best when I'm so energy depleted?

3. Your Mind: How are people with less intelligence than me experiencing success?

4. Spirituality: What's the balance between having faith and being delusional?

5. Eternal Influence: How will I invest in the future when I'm barely making it through each day now?

6. Loving Relationships: How do I get the people I care about to support my goals.?

7. Financial: Why don't I earn more money when I work harder than people with more than enough money?

The Now or Never Goal Program will answer these questions and help you, step-by-step, to reach your most important goals! There are three main barriers to success in the areas of Time, Health, Your Mind, Spirituality, Eternal Influence, Loving Relationships, and Finance. At the end of this 21-Day program, you will beam with the confidence that comes from breaking barriers that previously kept you at a sticking point.

## THE LACKING THREE
Through years of helping educators, students, and church members to reach their goals, I discovered three common barriers to success in each area of T.H.Y.S.E.L.F. These are called the lacking three:

1. Lack of Power
2. Lack of Planning
3. Lack of Progress

Your goals will be achieved when you eliminate the lack of power, lack of planning, and lack of progress in your daily routine. You only have to devote 21 minutes per day for 21-Days to reverse this trend!

## THE PLAN FOR BREAKING BARRIERS IN T.H.Y.S.E.L.F.

Your 21 day program will be divided into 7 three day modules. The first set of modules will provide the steps to eliminate lack of power. The second set of modules will provide the steps to eliminate lack of planning. The third set of modules will provide the steps to eliminate lack of progress.

# The Next 21-Days

*Time*
Day1: Power Module - Where Will You Be In 21 Days?
Day2: Planning Module - Distraction Proof!
Day3: Progress Module - Do It N.O.W.!

*Health*
Day 4: Power Module - Know Thy Body.
Day 5: Planning Module - How to Get Results!
Day 6: Progress Module - Unstoppable Energy!

*Your Mind*
Day 7: Power Module - What You Really Believe.
Day 8: Planning Module - Decide Today!
Day 9: Progress Module - Learning Life Lessons.

*Spirituality*
Day 10: Power Module -The Comfort Trap!
Day 11: Planning Module - A Matter of Time.
Day 12: Progress Module - Pay Attention!

*Eternal Influence*
Day 13: Power Module - Larger Than Life!
Day 14: Planning Module - Life Purpose.
Day 15: Progress Module - Living Your Legacy!

*Loving Relationships*
Day 16: Power Module - Relationship Power.
Day 17: Planning Module - Love For The Haters!
Day 18: Progress Module - Exponential Network!

*Financial*
Day 19: Power Module - Prosper In the New Economy!
Day 20: Planning Module - Mind over Money!
Day 21: Progress Module - Finance and Life Progress.

# How to Use This Program

### *The Root of Your Results*

During the next 21 days you will experience unexpected obstacles on your route to a new life. I always love to say, "Success isn't easy but somebody has to do it." You are that somebody! As we proceed, you will face obstacles that will make your goal appear impossible. Fear not! I'm going to teach you how to implement the "Sow in Private Principle." This principle simply states, "If you sow in private you will reap in public." Rightly applied, this principle will give you power over any visible challenge!

- This principle exists everywhere. Michael Jordan, Muhammad Ali, or Serena Williams will agree that practice dictates performance. Warren Buffet and Oprah Winfrey would agree that their mindset preceded their money. What you cannot see is much more potent than what you can see. Here's how we will apply this principle over the next 21 Days:

### *Your Daily Assignment*

You will be given a power principle along with an application exercise each day. The application exercise will give you time to think on paper. My friend Earl Davis says, "Millionaire's think on paper." While this principle can manifest itself in terms of financial gain; the principle applies to any area you wish to see desired results.

- Give yourself at least twenty one private minutes each day to read the power principle and work through the application exercise.

- You will begin to see great results as you answer the targeted questions and take the action steps! Together, we will advance in the direction of your goal! Investing twenty one minutes a day in your private life will manifest the results you want in your public life. Let's get started!!!

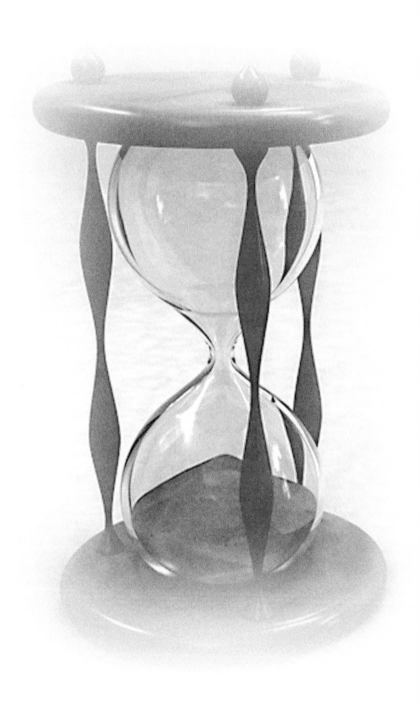

# 1
## TIME

*How to go from being busy to being focused!*

### DAY 1: WHERE WILL YOU BE IN 21 DAYS?

"Ask, and it shall be given unto you; seek, and ye shall find; knock, and it shall be opened unto you: for every one that asketh receiveth; and he that seeketh findeth; and to him that knocketh it shall be opened.".... Jesus Christ

Are you hesitant about a goal or opportunity that would be great for you? Perish the thought! From this day forward, success is your birthright. What specific dream would you like to realize over the next 21 days? You must believe that you have it while you are in the process of acquisition. Razor sharp focus will serve you well. Select a target, review it daily for the next three weeks, and make it happen! See you at the top!

# DAY 1 EXERCISES

1) List 4 accomplishments that would enhance the quality of your life.

A. _____

B. _____

C. _____

D. _____

2) Prioritize: Of the four goals you listed, which one would best position you to accomplish the other three?


3) List 2-3 reasons why you would like to accomplish this goal?

A. _____

B. _____

C. _____

## S.M.A.R.T. Goal

Write your priority goal from #2.

_____

Write an important milestone that would bring you closer to that achievement:

_____

## S.M.A.R.T. Goal funnel

### Specific Skill

- In what area will you develop new skill to reach your goal? I will develop my skill in _____ in order to help_____

### Measurable
- How will you know when your goal is reached? _____

  _____

- What will you use to measure progress?_____

### Attainable
- Identify the resources and personal contacts that can help you:_____

### Realistic 21-Day Target
- Can you reach this goal without compromising rest or relationshps?_____

### Time Certain
- Write the date you will achieve this goal:_____

Written S.M.A.R.T. Goal (Start goal statement with, "Through faith, I am happy and grateful that Jesus has blessed me to..." (state goal and include the date your goal will be achieved)

_____

_____

_____

_____

"This space is provided to write your goal down each day!
Next, read this motivational quote:"

*"Ask, and it shall be given unto you; seek, and ye shall find; knock, and it shall be opened unto you: for every one that asketh receiveth; and he that seeketh findeth; and to him that knocketh it shall be opened....."*

*Jesus Christ*

# DAY 2: DISTRACTION PROOF

"State awareness: being fully aware of what you can control or what you can't control and being fully focused on whatever you're doing in the moment is the single defining characteristic of the world's highest performers that I have ever met...This includes multiple world record holders in athletics, this includes billionaires...this singular type of focus is the only common characteristic that I have found with many differences among top performers".....Timothy Ferris being interviewed by Eben Pagan

It has often been said that success is the result of doing the right things at the right time. I would like to add that success is the result of giving our full attention to the right things at the right time. The ability to ignore distraction and stay focused will launch your productivity!

Distraction occurs when your momentum with a task is broken by something less important . In this case, you should simply ignore the distraction and move forward. Rarely will you be interrupted by something more important than a prioritized task. In the event you are, rotate your attention and give the gift of your entire presence. The wisest man that ever lived wrote, "Whatsoever thy hand findeth to do, do it with thy might." Complete the exercises for day 2 on the next page.

# DAY 2 EXERCISES

List the most common interruptions that prolong the time it takes you to complete something from start to finish.

_____

_____

List the interruptions that you enjoy.

_____

_____

Which of the above interruptions are life and death scenarios?

_____

_____

List 3 time consuming distractions that you can safely ignore over the next 20 Days.

    A. _____

    B. _____

    C. _____

Written S.M.A.R.T. Goal (Start goal statement with, "Through faith, I am happy and grateful that Jesus has blessed me to…" (state goal and include the date your goal will be achieved)

_____

_____

_____

_____

"This space is provided to write your goal down each day! Next, read this motivational quote:"

*"Ask, and it shall be given unto you; seek, and ye shall find; knock, and it shall be opened unto you: for every one that asketh receiveth; and he that seeketh findeth; and to him that knocketh it shall be opened….."*

*Jesus Christ*

# DAY 3: DO IT N.O.W.!

*"The time is always right to do what is right..."*
*Martin Luther King.*

Welcome to day 3 of your 21 day challenge!  The brevity of this program will require you to act instantly!  Review your goal several times each day.  This will result in unanticipated flashes of inspiration!  When this occurs, act on the inspiration immediately!  When you cannot act immediately, write down what you will do when you have the opportunity.  The act of writing your intentions will increase their likelihood of becoming reality!

Do it N.O.W. is an acronym that I learned from Stephen Pierce.  N.O.W. simply means, "No Opportunity Waits."  The longer you wait, the further inspiration will drift away from you.  Don't allow the windows of opportunity to close on you.  Go out and make it happen!  Complete your day 3 exercises on the next page.

## DAY 3 EXERCISES

1.  Keep a journal or file labeled, "Inspiration", in order to capture you best ideas and act on them.

2.  Write or type the six most important things you want to accomplish the next day, before you go to bed. In my experience, using a cell phone makes this process simple and practical. Download a to-do list application like awesome note or a free application designed for your cell phone.

    *   _____
    *   _____
    *   _____
    *   _____
    *   _____
    *   _____

\***Write 1 next to the most important goal. Write the number 2 beside the second most important goal. Continue in this fashion until you reach goal six. Tackle one goal at a time until you complete your list. Its okay if you only get 1-2 items completed! Your ability to prioritize and focus will build incredible momentum towards your goal. You can always rewrite incomplete items on the next day's list.

1.  _____
2.  _____
3.  _____
4.  _____
5.  _____
6.  _____

Written S.M.A.R.T. Goal (Start goal statement with, "Through faith, I am happy and grateful that Jesus has blessed me to…" (state goal and include the date your goal will be achieved)

_____

_____

_____

_____

"This space is provided to write your goal down each day!
Next, read this motivational quote:"

*"Ask, and it shall be given unto you; seek, and ye shall find; knock, and it shall be opened unto you: for every one that asketh receiveth; and he that seeketh findeth; and to him that knocketh it shall be opened....."*

*Jesus Christ*

9

# 2
# HEALTH

*How To Look and Feel Your Best!*

## DAY 4: KNOW THY BODY

*"Those who do not find time for exercise will
have to find time for illness...."*
*Earl of Derby*

Your body is the mechanism through which you will execute and experience success on your terms! Improving the physical image of your body should not be discredited as a vain aspiration. Pursuing an ideal body image is strong motivation to follow an otherwise dull regimen of eating and exercising. When done properly, cosmetic enhancement will aid the other factors of your health. There are healthy nutrition and exercise strategies for burning fat or building muscle.

Today I will help you experience one cosmetic health benefit. You will be provided with a plan to accompany your choice. Here are your choices:

1.  Add muscle to my frame(http://www.billpearl.com/bpprograms.asp)
2.  Trim fat from my frame(http://www.fasttrackfatloss.com)

The above options will ignite the energy required to reach your most important goal! As an added bonus, you will look great! Your day 4 exercises are on the next page.

## DAY 4 EXERCISES

Today's exercise requires a simple decision. While many desire to build muscle and burn fat simultaneously, this is counterproductive in terms of selecting a meal plan. You have to follow a nutrition plan that does one or the other in order to see effective physical results.

Circle the meal plan that would align best with your body transformation goal.
  A. Fat loss meal plan
  B. Muscle building meal plan.

Here are two resources that will help you achieve fat loss or muscle building:

*1-NON-VEGETARIAN RESOURCE*
Dave Ruel has designed a program with tasty, simple recipes for burning fat or building muscle. Here is the url to his e-book: http://www.anaboliccooking.com/welcome/index.php?hop=grothyself:

*2-VEGETARIAN RESOURCE*
Robert Cheeke has written a book with numerous meal plans suited for vegetarians who wish to burn fat or build muscle. Though I disagree with his spiritual philosophy, the recipes and meal plans are solid! Here is the web address to order his book: http://www.amazon.com/Vegan-Bodybuilding-Fitness-Robert-Cheeke/dp/0984391606

Making this decision may seem unrelated to your goal now. Nevertheless, your energy level is critical to taking action on your goal. Also, greater health and confidence will only expedite the process of reaching your goal. See you on day 5!

Written S.M.A.R.T. Goal (Start goal statement with, "Through faith, I am happy and grateful that Jesus has blessed me to…" (state goal and include the date your goal will be achieved)

_____

_____
_____

_____

"This space is provided to write your goal down each day!
Next, read this motivational quote:"

*"Ask, and it shall be given unto you; seek, and ye shall find; knock, and it shall be opened unto you: for every one that asketh receiveth; and he that seeketh findeth; and to him that knocketh it shall be opened….."*

*Jesus Christ*

# DAY 5: HOW TO GET RESULTS

*"Work joyfully and peacefully, knowing that right thoughts and right efforts will inevitably bring about right results......"*
*James Allen*

Albert Einstein defined insanity as doing the same thing over and over again and expecting different results. While I agree, the cognitive aspect of this principle is often overlooked. Success begins at the level of thought. Here is the new definition of insanity: Thinking the same thing and expecting to get different results. Your health goal will remain a desire without replacing outdated beliefs with new and factual information. What areas would you like to learn more about as it relates to your health?

(Example: As part of my Day 5 commitment, I will learn more about nutrition).

The decision is yours to make. Your energy is the mechanism through which you conquer this 21-Day challenge! Select habits that will invigorate you toward that end!

## DAY 5 EXERCISES

The ironic truth is that the more you know, the more you realize what you don't know. When it comes to boosting your energy, there is always more to learn. Today, you will gain the psychological advantage of signing a personal commitment.

Complete the following statement: In order to build energy toward my S.M.A.R.T. Goal; I will learn more about _____.

    Signature_____

    Today's Date_____

Written S.M.A.R.T. Goal (Start goal statement with, "Through faith, I am happy and grateful that Jesus has blessed me to…" (state goal and include the date your goal will be achieved)

_____

_____

_____

_____

"This space is provided to write your goal down each day!
Next, read this motivational quote:"

*"Ask, and it shall be given unto you; seek, and ye shall find; knock, and it shall be opened unto you: for every one that asketh receiveth; and he that seeketh findeth; and to him that knocketh it shall be opened....."*

*Jesus Christ*

# DAY 6: UNSTOPPABLE ENERGY!

*"The key to being unstoppable is to not stop..."*
Brian Tracy

Challenges await you at every realm of progress. This is particularly true when it comes to your energy level. Nonetheless, you can pierce the barrier of your current energy level! Though obstacles lie ahead, you cannot be stopped when you plant one foot in front of the other. Your success is certain when you persist daily. For the past two days, you learned fitness and nutrition principles that move you toward your goal. However, this section would be incomplete without addressing the epidemic of "restlessness." Nothing is more counterproductive than a workaholic approach to your goal. Without rest or recovery, your body will respond with numerous health and beauty ailments.

Recovery is the most overlooked area of energy. According to Tony Schwartz, your productivity will boost when you work in 90 minute blocks of focused activity. Next, have a brief period of renewal. He wrote an excellent article for Harvard Business Review entitled, "How To Recover Your Core Rhythm." He noted that top performing athletes and musicians average 8.5 hours of sleep per day! If that seems too unpractical, a 30-minute nap can recharge you for upcoming activities. Paradoxically, taking time to stop will make you unstoppable! Let's meet again tomorrow!

# DAY 6 EXERCISES

Planning your time wisely will amplify your energy. Also, following through on the nutrition principles from day 4 will literally feed your productivity. Today you will experiment with the 90 minute productivity principle. Here are your two action steps:

Step 1: Write down your top three priorities today

Priority 1 _____
Priority 2 _____
Priority 3 _____

Step 2: Assign separate 90 minute blocks to each priority. Give yourself plenty of space between each 90 minute block. You will be surprised at the quality of energy you bring to each 90 minute block.

Examples:
9:00-10:30: Return e-mails and schedule appointments for next week.
12:30-2:00: Work on presentation for next week's training.
5:00-6:30: Drive to the gym and exercise for one hour.

Written S.M.A.R.T. Goal (Start goal statement with, "Through faith, I am happy and grateful that Jesus has blessed me to…" (state goal and include the date your goal will be achieved)

_____

_____

_____

_____

"This space is provided to write your goal down each day! Next, read this motivational quote:"

*"Ask, and it shall be given unto you; seek, and ye shall find; knock, and it shall be opened unto you: for every one that asketh receiveth; and he that seeketh findeth; and to him that knocketh it shall be opened....."*

*Jesus Christ*

# 3
# YOUR MIND

*How To Use Your Mind To Yield Positive Results*

## DAY 7: WHAT YOU REALLY BELIEVE

*"If thou canst believe, all things are possible to him that believeth."*
*..Jesus Christ*

You should be commended for pursuing a single goal thus far in the challenge. As you read your goal each day, consider the role of belief. The average person will aim for what they believe they can accomplish versus what they really want. When this is the case, you must break the barrier of unbelief. Speak your goal out loud and have confidence in its fulfillment. I'm serious, speak it out loud! When God's will and your will connect; nothing on earth can stop you!

When your thoughts shift toward belief, the world will bend over backwards to assist you. People love to say, "I will believe it when I see it." Nothing could be further from the truth! In reality, "you will see it when you believe it." It's time to dust off your dreams and start playing to win!

## DAY 7 EXERCISES

Go to Google images and find pictures that visually represent your S.M.A.R.T. Goal. Copy and paste these images to a page in microsoft word. Print the page and place it where you will have a daily view of the end you are striving toward.

.

Written S.M.A.R.T. Goal (Start goal statement with, "Through faith, I am happy and grateful that Jesus has blessed me to…" (state goal and include the date your goal will be achieved)

_____
_____
_____
_____

"This space is provided to write your goal down each day!
Next, read this motivational quote:"

_"Ask, and it shall be given unto you; seek, and ye shall find; knock, and it shall be opened unto you: for every one that asketh receiveth; and he that seeketh findeth; and to him that knocketh it shall be opened….."_

_Jesus Christ_

# DAY 8: DECIDE TODAY!

*" The strongest principle of growth lies in human choice."*
*George Elliot*

The purpose of life is growth. Your best decisions are choices that promote your progress. Conversely, an option that inhibits your growth is a step in the wrong direction. If you have the opportunity to grow, go for it!

# DAY 8 EXERCISES

There are so many non-essentials in life that steal our time, space, and energy. Overcrowded schedules, e-mails, closets, and mental space leave little capacity to expand.

Decide what you can eliminate from the following areas of your life:

*Schedule:*_____

*E-mail lists:*_____

*Memberships:*_____

*Clothing:*_____

*UnhealthyAcquaintances:*_____

*Television/Cable Shows:*_____

*Unhealthy foods:*_____

*Things I can give away:*_____

Written S.M.A.R.T. Goal (Start goal statement with, "Through faith, I am happy and grateful that Jesus has blessed me to…" (state goal and include the date your goal will be achieved)

_____

_____
_____

_____

"This space is provided to write your goal down each day!
Next, read this motivational quote:"

_"Ask, and it shall be given unto you; seek, and ye shall find; knock, and it shall be opened unto you: for every one that asketh receiveth; and he that seeketh findeth; and to him that knocketh it shall be opened....."_

_Jesus Christ_

# DAY 9: LEARNING LIFE LESSONS

*"I don't think much of a man who is not wiser today*
*than he was yesterday."*
Abraham Lincoln

Knowledge only represents potential learning. True learning is accompanied by behavior change. In school, you learned a lesson that was followed by a test. In life, you have tests that are followed by lessons. That's good news! The minute you adapt, a new test awaits you. Life is only boring when you repeat the same test over and over.

## DAY 9 EXERCISES

What is the most frustrating circumstance you seem to face over, and over, and over again!! Think of something that bugs you to no end!!

What new habit will you form to make sure this stops happening!

_____

Write the benefit of forming this new habit?

_____

Write the tragedy of neglecting this new habit?

_____

Written S.M.A.R.T. Goal (Start goal statement with, "Through faith, I am happy and grateful that Jesus has blessed me to..." (state goal and include the date your goal will be achieved)

_____

_____
_____

_____

"This space is provided to write your goal down each day! Next, read this motivational quote:"

*"Ask, and it shall be given unto you; seek, and ye shall find; knock, and it shall be opened unto you: for every one that asketh receiveth; and he that seeketh findeth; and to him that knocketh it shall be opened....."*

*Jesus Christ*

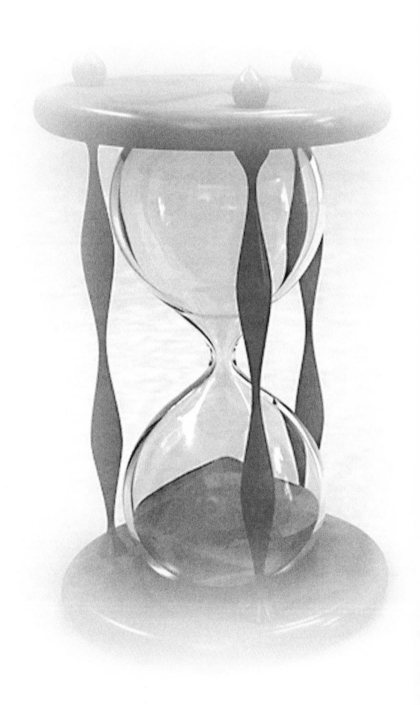

# 4
# SPIRITUALITY

*How To Build Belief and Take Action!*

### DAY 10: THE COMFORT TRAP

*"The truth is that our finest moments are most likely to occur when we are feeling deeply uncomfortable, unhappy, or unfulfilled. For it is only in such moments, propelled by our discomfort, that we are likely to step out of our ruts and start searching for different ways."*
M. Scott Peck

It is quite natural to fear moving in a direction that will harm you. Ironically, it is also natural to fear moving in a direction that will help you! Every step toward your progress will be accompanied by an initial feeling of discomfort. The mediocre interpret this feeling as a signal to halt or slow down. Your mediocre days are over! The successful are those who seize discomfort and run with it! Form the habit of being comfortable with the uncomfortable and your personal growth will explode!

# DAY 10 EXERCISES

List actions that would be good for your goal, yet you talked yourself out of them:_____

_____

Today I want to introduce you to the F.T.F. principle. F.T.F. is an acronym for, "Feared Things First." Generally, everything you want in life is on the other side of fear.

In relation to your goal, write the activity which creates the most anxiety:

_____

_____

Now that you have identified this activity, make it your number one priority today!

Does that make you uncomfortable? Great, it's supposed to! How else are you going to grow? Not only will you grow, the anxiety will be eliminated after you finish. As a bonus, you will have more energy to tackle the rest of your activities!

Most people do things in the opposite order. As a result, they devote less energy to actions that would transform their lives!

Form the habit of being comfortable with the uncomfortable. Imagine what would happen if you formed the F.T.F. habit each day! Your growth, emotional freedom, and happiness would soar!

Written S.M.A.R.T. Goal (Start goal statement with, "Through faith, I am happy and grateful that Jesus has blessed me to…" (state goal and include the date your goal will be achieved)

_____

_____

_____

_____

"This space is provided to write your goal down each day!
Next, read this motivational quote:"

*"Ask, and it shall be given unto you; seek, and ye shall find;
knock, and it shall be opened unto you: for every one that asketh
receiveth; and he that seeketh findeth; and to him that knocketh it
shall be opened….."*

*Jesus Christ*

# DAY 11: INEVITABLE SUCCESS

*"Every day is a gift, and how you use it brings you either one day closer to or one day farther from your goal."*
*Jim Stovall*

Conrad Hilton is best known for his successful chain of Hilton Hotels. One day he was approached by a reporter who asked, "When did you know you would be successful?" Mr. Hilton told the reporter he knew he would succeed when he was homeless and sleeping on a park bench. At that time, he learned habits which led to his personal success. Do you have the mindset, motivation, and habits of someone who has reached your personal goal? If so, you are already a success. If not, I will help you develop a plan on the next page!

## DAY 11 EXERCISES

Nothing happens overnight. As Jim Stovall wrote, "Success is not a one size fits all proposition." When the farmer plants a seed, there are many factors involved in the process of that plant maturing. The farmer will do harm by rushing that process. Likewise, you planted a goal on the first day of this process. During times of frustration and impatience you will be tempted to take actions that are counterproductive. Whether the temptation is to spend more, eat more, work more, or take a side track; the result is this: Impatient action delays your desired result. There is only so much work you can do. Remember the adage, "less is more."

Answer the following questions:

What am I doing that should not be done?

_____

_____

What can I do to regain my focus when I am thrown off track?

_____

_____

Written S.M.A.R.T. Goal (Start goal statement with, "Through faith, I am happy and grateful that Jesus has blessed me to…" (state goal and include the date your goal will be achieved)

_____

_____

_____

_____

"This space is provided to write your goal down each day! Next, read this motivational quote:"

*"Ask, and it shall be given unto you; seek, and ye shall find; knock, and it shall be opened unto you: for every one that asketh receiveth; and he that seeketh findeth; and to him that knocketh it shall be opened....."*

*Jesus Christ*

## DAY 12:PAY ATTENTION

*"If you don't get it in the whisper, then a brick will fall on your head. If you don't get it when the brick falls on your head, the wall comes falling down. If you don't get it when the wall comes down, the whole house collapses. The key is to get it in the whisper."*
*Oprah Winfrey*


Think of your immediate goal. You will naturally meet with obstacles along the journey. As you progress, there will be subtle evidence that attainment is within your grasp. Pay attention to the signals that tell you to keep striving, keep waiting, keep learning, and keep growing!

## DAY 12 EXERCISES

When you are inches short of a goal, challenges arise from multiple angles. In this instance, what is happening inside of you is more powerful than what is happening outside of you! Guess what occurs when your inner faith becomes bigger than your outward challenge? You conquer every test! I would like to leave you with two words as you contemplate today's action step: CHOOSE FAITH!

What circumstances are you facing that cause you to doubt the possibility of your goal?

_____

_____

_____.


The circumstances that you listed are best viewed as tests of your faith. As the ancient text reads, "With men it is impossible, With God all things are possible.

Disappointments are a test of faith. How can you best respond to the circumstances that tempt you to halt progress?

_____

_____

_____.

Written S.M.A.R.T. Goal (Start goal statement with, "Through faith, I am happy and grateful that Jesus has blessed me to…" (state goal and include the date your goal will be achieved)

_____

_____

_____

_____

"This space is provided to write your goal down each day!
Next, read this motivational quote:"

_"Ask, and it shall be given unto you; seek, and ye shall find; knock, and it shall be opened unto you: for every one that asketh receiveth; and he that seeketh findeth; and to him that knocketh it shall be opened....."_

_Jesus Christ_

# 5

# ETERNAL INFLUENCE

*How To Live and Give Your Legacy!*

### DAY 13 : LARGER THAN LIFE

*"And this is life eternal, that they might know thee the only true God,
and Jesus Christ, whom thou hast sent."*
*Jesus Christ*

You can be in perfect harmony with the God of this universe. The only hindrance to your harmony with God is an experience the bible refers to as sin. By definition, sin is the violation of God's law. Unfortunately, death is the inevitable result of violating His law: "For the wages of sin is death (Romans 6:23)." This explains the purpose of Jesus Christ's death.

The biography of Jesus Christ entitled, "Desire of Ages," describes the function of His death in this statement: "Christ was treated as we deserve, that we might be treated as He deserves. He was condemned for our sins, in which He had no share, that we might be justified by His righteousness in which we had no share. He suffered the death which was ours, that we might receive the life which was His." Historical and biblical writers confirm that Jesus Christ rose from the dead after suffering death on a cross.

The power that enabled Christ to rise from the dead is available to you! Christ stated in his own words, "Therefore doth my Father love me, because I lay down my life, that I might take it again. No man taketh it from me, but I lay it down of myself. I have power to lay it down, and I have power to take it again (John 10:17, 18)." Day 13 exercises will show you how to employ this type of power in your daily life!

# DAY 13 EXERCISES

You invite supernatural power into your life when you apply the wisdom found in scripture.

Select one area where you need extra power in relation to your goal. Next, write down how you will apply the scriptural advice in that particular area:

A. Taking Advice: Psalms 1:1-3, Proverbs 15:22
   Application: _____

   _____

   _____.

B. Making Plans: Psalms 20:4, Proverbs 16:3
   Application:_____

   _____

   _____.

C. Patience: Proverbs 28:20, 1 Thessalonians 5:14
   Application:_____

   _____

   _____.

D. Personality: Proverbs 22:4
   Application:_____

   _____

   _____.

Written S.M.A.R.T. Goal (Start goal statement with, "Through faith, I am happy and grateful that Jesus has blessed me to…" (state goal and include the date your goal will be achieved)

_____

_____

_____

_____

"This space is provided to write your goal down each day! Next, read this motivational quote:"

*"Ask, and it shall be given unto you; seek, and ye shall find; knock, and it shall be opened unto you: for every one that asketh receiveth; and he that seeketh findeth; and to him that knocketh it shall be opened....."*

*Jesus Christ*

# DAY 14 : LIFE PURPOSE

*"Here is the test to find whether your mission on earth is finished.*
*If you're alive, it isn't."*
*Richard Bach*

When you are connected to the God who is larger than life, you can fulfill a calling that is larger than life. Yes, God has a plan and purpose for your life! Many people try to get God to cosign on their personal agenda rather than receive the one He has already designed. His plan will bring you happiness and peace throughout the days of your life. Understanding how your current goal fits within a larger context will propel you forward. Day 14 exercises will lead you through a process that will help you discover your niche in life!

## DAY 14 EXERCISES

List the most challenging struggles that you have overcome in life. Feel free to add age ranges.

From ages 1-10

_____

From ages 10-20

_____

From ages 20-30

_____

From ages 30-40

_____

From ages 40-50

_____

From ages 50-60

_____

What common thread do you notice in the challenges you have over-come?

You have overcome these struggles in order to be a voice for people who need to rise above similar challenges. What target groups of people are struggling with the challenges you have overcome? _____

_____.

Use your talents and skills to serve these groups. This is your lifework.

Written S.M.A.R.T. Goal (Start goal statement with, "Through faith, I am happy and grateful that Jesus has blessed me to…" (state goal and include the date your goal will be achieved)

_____

_____

_____

_____

"This space is provided to write your goal down each day!
Next, read this motivational quote:"

*"Ask, and it shall be given unto you; seek, and ye shall find; knock, and it shall be opened unto you: for every one that asketh receiveth; and he that seeketh findeth; and to him that knocketh it shall be opened….."*

*Jesus Christ*

# DAY 15 : LIVING YOUR LEGACY

"For the past 33 years, I have looked in the mirror every morning
and asked myself: "If today were the last day of my life, would I
want to do what I am about to do today?" And whenever the answer
has been "No" for too many days in a row, I know I need to change
something...almost everything - all external expectations, all pride,
all fear of embarrassment or failure - these things just fall away in the
face of death, leaving only what is truly important. Remembering that
you are going to die is the best way I know to avoid the trap of
thinking you have something to lose."
Steve Jobs

On day 14, you clarified a purpose that will make this world better for
you and those within your circle of influence. You are in charge of the
preparation. God is in charge of the opportunities. As you prepare,
there is a role that providence plays in your life. Some people call it
chance. However, the evidence in our world suggests that everything
in life is by design. Even obstacles play a role in helping your purpose
come to fruition. As Byron Katie stated, "Life gives you everything
you need." Accepting small adaptations will allow you to witness the
daily unfolding of a larger legacy.

Day 15 exercises will help you approach your 21 Day goal with a process that allows room for divine intervention. As a result, your response to life will carry eternal influence.

# DAY 15 EXERCISES

The following three steps are habits that I practice each day. Try each step and write down your impressions on the blank lines.

Step 1: Acknowledge that you are a child of God and ask him for wisdom through prayer and inspiring bible scriptures.

_____

_____

_____.


Step 2: Make plans (see day 3 in Chapter 1) and trust that God will provide the means for them to be carried out or cancelled. Trust, that He has your best interest in mind.

_____

_____

_____.


Step 3: Pray to be a vessel that God will use today. Ask Him to be with you.

_____

_____

_____.

Written S.M.A.R.T. Goal (Start goal statement with, "Through faith, I am happy and grateful that Jesus has blessed me to…" (state goal and include the date your goal will be achieved)

_____

_____

_____

_____

"This space is provided to write your goal down each day! Next, read this motivational quote:"

*"Ask, and it shall be given unto you; seek, and ye shall find; knock, and it shall be opened unto you: for every one that asketh receiveth; and he that seeketh findeth; and to him that knocketh it shall be opened….."*

*Jesus Christ*

# 6
# LOVING RELATIONSHIPS

*How To Improve Your Relationships!*

### DAY 16 : RELATIONSHIP POWER

*"To live we must conquer incessantly,*
*we must have the courage to be happy."*
*Henri Frederic Amiel*

Positive and negative relationships are part of the human experience. Thankfully, your happiness is determined by your response to these relationships. Pastor Joel Osteen shared that one of his members approached him with the following dilemma: "Pastor, if I had a man I would be happy." Two months later she approached him and said, "Pastor, if I could get rid of this man I would be happy." The belief that happiness will come from another human being is at the foundation of many dysfunctional relationships.

 Your happiness is not dependent on another person. It is dependent on your progress along the various spheres of life. Personal progress will enhance your current relationships while setting the stage for new connections!

Your personal fulfillment is the starting point for engaging in healthy relationships. Today's exercises will help you experience happiness in your current relationships by increasing your personal fulfillment!

## DAY 16 EXERCISES

Write what you are dissatisfied with in the following areas:

1. Physical  (examples: low energy, little to no muscle tone, etc.)

   _____

   _____

2. Mental  (examples: poor memory, little knowledge in some critical area, poor decision making, limited creativity, etc.)

   _____

   _____

3. Spiritual  (examples: inadequate prayer life, supersize ego, unacquainted with the bible and other inspirational literature, too busy to serve others, uncharitable, etc.):

   _____

   _____

4. Social  (examples: unfocused listener, more manipulative than persuasive, void of empathy, limited vocabulary, frequent mis understandings with spouse, poor boundaries, socially rigid, etc.)

   _____

   _____

Written S.M.A.R.T. Goal (Start goal statement with, "Through faith, I am happy and grateful that Jesus has blessed me to..." (state goal and include the date your goal will be achieved)

_____

_____

_____

_____

"This space is provided to write your goal down each day!
Next, read this motivational quote:"

*"Ask, and it shall be given unto you; seek, and ye shall find; knock, and it shall be opened unto you: for every one that asketh receiveth; and he that seeketh findeth; and to him that knocketh it shall be opened....."*

*Jesus Christ*

# DAY 17 : LOVE FOR THE HATERS

*"If the world hate you, ye know that it hated me before it hated you. If ye were of the world, the world would love his own: but because ye are not of this world, but I have chosen you out of the world, therefore the world hateth you."*
*Jesus Christ*


Yesterday, you took action toward your personal progress. This progress will come with an initial feeling of discomfort. Keep taking the necessary actions. Your success demands you proceed in spite of uneasiness. Accepting this process allows you to walk a path of perpetual growth. On another note, let's consider the discomfort of your family and friends when you start to grow.

You have family and friends who have become comfortable with the way you were. Whenever you grow, they become uncomfortable also. This is not always due to jealousy or insincerity. They are simply not ready to analyze themselves the way you have in order to move forward. When you change, they sense that you will eventually part ways. Are you willing to walk out of the shadow of others to become who you were meant to be? If so, you will continue to experience new levels of success! Day 17 exercises will help you develop a plan to put things in perspective.

# DAY 17 EXERCISES

Your goal has caused an emotional difference in you and your relationships. List a few people that have been emotionally affected by your path of progress:

    1._____

    2._____

    3._____

    4._____

    5._____

List the things you continue to appreciate about them?

_____

_____

_____.

List any new boundaries you must set around your associations in order to continue making progress (Examples: Limit phone conversations with\_\_\_\_\_, spend less time with\_\_\_\_).

_____

_____

_____.

Appreciate the best and put boundaries around the rest. There are redeeming qualities in the worst of us and negative qualities in the best of us. Accept things for what they are and continue moving forward.

Written S.M.A.R.T. Goal (Start goal statement with, "Through faith, I am happy and grateful that Jesus has blessed me to..." (state goal and include the date your goal will be achieved)

_____

_____

_____

_____

"This space is provided to write your goal down each day!
Next, read this motivational quote:"

*"Ask, and it shall be given unto you; seek, and ye shall find; knock, and it shall be opened unto you: for every one that asketh receiveth; and he that seeketh findeth; and to him that knocketh it shall be opened....."*

*Jesus Christ*

# DAY 18 : EXPONENTIAL NETWORKING

*"The way of the world is meeting people through other people."*
*Robert Kerrigan*

Networking is one of the key factors of success. Offer value to the network of others and they will share their value with your network. A networking exchange should result in both parties having a referral for each other. This may or may not include you personally. Every person you meet is a gateway to hundreds of new connections. Likewise, you empower your network by introducing them to new people of value. The ebb and flow of this system works beautifully. Day 18 exercises will help you apply the principles of networking to your current goal. Likewise, the principles you learn will serve you in the future. Stay connected!

# DAY 18 EXERCISES

Here is the most common question you will be asked when meeting a new professional acquaintance: "What do you do?" Wouldn't it be nice if you answered this question in a way that connected you and your new acquaintance?

Here is a fill in the blank formula that was introduced to me through Brendon Bruchard's, "Total Product Blueprint." Complete the following statement:

I HELP _____ (your target audience)
UNDERSTAND_____ (Topic)
SO THAT (Benefit to the target audience)

I will use myself as an example. Hello, my name is Ryan Jeffery. I help Christian believers reach their personal goals so that they can experience greater peace, health, and happiness!

Written S.M.A.R.T. Goal (Start goal statement with, "Through faith, I am happy and grateful that Jesus has blessed me to…" (state goal and include the date your goal will be achieved)

_____

_____

_____

_____

"This space is provided to write your goal down each day!
Next, read this motivational quote:"

_"Ask, and it shall be given unto you; seek, and ye shall find; knock, and it shall be opened unto you: for every one that asketh receiveth; and he that seeketh findeth; and to him that knocketh it shall be opened....."_

_Jesus Christ_

# 7
# FINANCE

*How to profit by strengthening your strengths!*

## DAY 19 : PROSPER IN THE NEW ECONOMY

*"The illiterate of the 21st century will not be those who cannot read or write, but those who cannot learn, unlearn, and relearn."*
*Alvin Toffler*

There are financial implications to the goal you have set for yourself during this 21-Day cycle. Some goals are limited by financial restrictions. Knowing how to prosper in this economy is critical to your continued progress. We live in a knowledge-based economy. Yet, many are operating with an industrial based mindset. The same thing happened during the great depression. The agricultural based economy suffered while the industrial based economy started to boom!

Now the industrial based economy is on life support while the knowledge economy is booming! We live in a time where you can profit from your passion! This process is unveiled in books like, "Get Paid For Who You Are" by David Wood and "Millionaire Messenger" by Brendon Bruchard.

On the next page, I will introduce you to a complimentary training where you will learn how to profit from your passion. You are passionate about certain topics, right? Today's exercises will help you move from passion to profit!

## DAY 19 EXERCISES

1. Watch a free video training on how you can profit from your expertise here: http://www.totalproductblueprint.com. Whether you realize it or not, you are an expert. This training will help you learn how to profit from your passion.

2. How will what you just learned contribute to your current goal?

   _____

   _____

   _____

   _____

3. After watching the training, what ideas do you have about using your passion to gain financial strength?

   _____

   _____

   _____

   _____

Remember, it's not about how many resources you have, it's about how resourceful you are!

Written S.M.A.R.T. Goal (Start goal statement with, "Through faith, I am happy and grateful that Jesus has blessed me to…" (state goal and include the date your goal will be achieved)

_____

_____

_____

_____

"This space is provided to write your goal down each day! Next, read this motivational quote:"

*"Ask, and it shall be given unto you; seek, and ye shall find; knock, and it shall be opened unto you: for every one that asketh receiveth; and he that seeketh findeth; and to him that knocketh it shall be opened....."*

*Jesus Christ*

# DAY 20 : MIND OVER MONEY

*"People first, then money, then things."*
*Suze Orman*

Dr. Thomas J. Stanley has studied millionaires for over 30 years. His data ranged from national surveys with 944 millionaire respondents and the Internal Revenue Service (the I.R.S has the best data in the world on millionaires). What he uncovered will challenge most perceptions of the financially elite. Here is what he found:

## *HOUSING*
Three times more millionaires live in homes valued at under 300,000 than over 1,000,000.

## *CLOTHING*
Six stores from the top ten stores patronized by millionaire men the most are as follows: Kohl's, Target, Costco, Wal-Mart, T.J. Maxx

Six stores from the top ten stores patronized by millionaire women are as follows: Ann Taylor, Macy's, Target, T.J. Maxx, Talbots, & Costco

## *VEHICLES*
The Toyota was found to be number one in market share among both millionaires and engineers in general. The most popular models were the Camry V6, Avalon, & Highlander. The Honda was a close second.

## *DINNER & RESTAURANTS*
The average price paid by over 90% of millionaires for their dinner at the Restaurant they dine at most frequently was $11.79

## HAIRCUT
More than 90% of millionaires paid under $15 for their last haircut (tip included).
Males- $9.34
Females- $14.85

## WATCHES
Seiko is the watch owned most frequently by millionaires. Rolex is the second. However, 46% of survey respondents who owned a Rolex received it as a gift.

## RELATIONSHIPS
59% of millionaires are married and have never been divorced.

Obviously, their value is not derived from their ability to buy expensive things. Spending outside of our range is a dead giveaway that we are overcompensating for a lack of personal worth. Besides, true success cannot be purchased. You must become a success and continue to become more successful. You will be doing the world and your wallet a favor! Today's exercises will help you gain the mental leverage required to make a plan for your money.

## DAY 20 EXERCISES

What is the most common emotion you experience about your money?

- A.  Stress
- B.  Fun
- C.  Neutral
- D.  Security
- E.  Guilt

Anne Kevitt has been a successful Entrepreneur and millionaire maker for several years. She noticed one common financial trait among the financially successful: They view money as a commodity! They are emotionally neutral about money. Most people have strong emotional attachments to money. For example, they are afraid they cannot get out of debt, they shop to make themselves feel better, or they feel superior to others when they drive expensive cars and wear brand name clothes, etc...Money is a thing, not an emotion. You can genuinely take charge of money when you are emotionally neutral toward it.

1.  What financial setback or mistake have you experienced that you must forgive yourself or someone else for?

   _____

2.  Create a phrase that you will tell yourself to regain perspective when emotions around money overwhelm you.

   _____

3.  Go to http://www.moneysavingchallenge.com/free-budget-template/ and download a simple wealth building budget plan.

Written S.M.A.R.T. Goal (Start goal statement with, "Through faith, I am happy and grateful that Jesus has blessed me to…" (state goal and include the date your goal will be achieved)

_____

_____

_____

_____

"This space is provided to write your goal down each day!
Next, read this motivational quote:"

_"Ask, and it shall be given unto you; seek, and ye shall find; knock, and it shall be opened unto you: for every one that asketh receiveth; and he that seeketh findeth; and to him that knocketh it shall be opened....."_

_Jesus Christ_

# DAY 21 : FINANCE AND LIFE PROGRESS

*"I have not failed, I've just found 10,000 ways that won't work"*
*Thomas A. Edison*

Congratulations for making it to Day 21!! You are a better person for making it to this point, no matter what you have or have not accomplished. I would like to make a brief point about money and progress. While money isn't the most important thing in life, it surely impacts everything that is important. No matter your goal, financial progress can always add to your success.

The past twenty days were only the beginning of your new life. As you probably know, it takes twenty one days to form a new habit. Your success in life is the result of habit. Most things that are gained quickly are lost just as fast. Lottery winners have a history of losing their money rapidly. People who diet hop blow up like blimps. The list goes on but the cause is the same: failing to align who we are with what we want.

You started this journey with one goal that was important to you. In the process, you learned habits required to accomplish this goal. Continue to practice these habits and your goal will certainly follow. If not today, it will come when you are ready. Never lose faith! Hopefully, you enjoyed our journey together! I am grateful that you provided me with the opportunity to be your coach. Repeat this 21 day process as often as you would like!

# DAY 21 EXERCISES

Written S.M.A.R.T. Goal (Start goal statement with, "Through faith, I am happy and grateful that Jesus has blessed me to..." (state goal to be achieved)

_____

_____

_____.


Did you meet your 21 Day target?  Circle One.
- A.  Yes
- B.  Not Yet
- C.  Realigned my priorities and discovered a new goal in the process.

What did you learn that will give you momentum in the next goal challenge you attempt?

_____

_____

_____.


What new habits did you incorporate into your lifestyle?

_____

_____

_____.


If you finished this 21 day process, you are a success.  Success is based on principles that are bigger than our mere imaginings.  Commitment to the process of success and persistence will always be rewarded.  Reward yourself in some way for completing a journey that most people avoid.  Celebrate!!!!!

**CONGRATULATIONS
ON COMPLETING
YOUR FIRST 21-DAY JOURNEY!!**

*"The more you praise and celebrate your life,
the more there is in life to celebrate."*

*Oprah Winfrey*

*THE END....FOR TODAY!*

## APPENDIX: Now or Never Goal Form

Write the goal you would like to reach at the end of your
21-Day Challenge.:

Now, run your goal through our S.M.A.R.T Goal Funnel:

Specific Skill
- In what area will you develop new skill to reach your goal?
  I will develop my skill in _____ in order to help_____

Measurable
- How will you know when your goal is reached?

  _____

- What will you use to measure progress?

  _____

Attainable
- Identify the resources and personal contacts that can help
  you.

  _____

Realistic 21-Day Target
- Can you reach this goal without compromising rest or
  relationships?

  _____

Time Certain
- Write the date you will achieve this goal.

  _____

Written S.M.A.R.T. Goal (Start goal statement with, "Through faith, I am happy and grateful that Jesus has blessed me to…" (state goal and include the date your goal will be achieved)

_____

_____

_____

_____

_____

_____

_____

# About the Author

Ryan is a behavior specialist for Fairfax County Public Schools. He has held several leadership roles in the fields of education and church ministry. He discovered how he and others could reach goals without sacrificing their health or relationships. He is particularly adept at helping Christian professionals multiply their results by achieving one important goal every 21 days!

*www.ryanjefferyonline.com*

# NOTES

# NOTES

# NOTES

# NOTES

# NOTES

# NOTES

# NOTES

# NOTES

# NOTES

# NOTES

# NOTES

**SPIRIT REIGN**
PUBLISHING
A Division of Spirit Reign Communications